HAUNTED HISTORY OF THE UNITED STATES

THE HAUNTED HISTORY OF GETTYSBURG, PENNSYLVANIA

BY HEATHER C. HUDAK

Core Library
An Imprint of Abdo Publishing
abdobooks.com

Cover image: Around 630 cannons were used during the Battle of Gettysburg. Today, hundreds of cannons still stand on the former battlefield.

abdobooks.com

Published by Abdo Publishing, a division of ABDO, PO Box 398166, Minneapolis, Minnesota 55439.

Printed in the United States of America, North Mankato, Minnesota.
102023
012024

THIS BOOK CONTAINS RECYCLED MATERIALS

Cover Photo: H. Abernathy/ClassicStock/Alamy
Interior Photos: HUM Images/Universal Images Group/Getty Images, 4–5; Bob Pool/Shutterstock Images, 6; Gary Saxe/Shutterstock Images, 10–11, 43; Karyl Miller/Shutterstock Images, 13, 45; Bill Dowling/Shutterstock Images, 15; Education Images/Universal Images Group/Getty Images, 18–19; Krumpeiman Photography/Shutterstock Images, 20; Shutterstock Images, 24, 26–27, 31, 39 (ghosts); Christian Hinkle/Shutterstock Images, 29; Red Line Editorial, 33; Mihai Andritoiu/Shutterstock Images, 34–35; Denis Maliugin/Shutterstock Images, 39 (head); Chronicle/Alamy, 39 (bottom)

Editors: Marie Pearson and Haley Williams
Series Designer: Ryan Gale

Library of Congress Control Number: 2023939624

Publisher's Cataloging-in-Publication Data
Names: Hudak, Heather C., author.
Title: The haunted history of Gettysburg, Pennsylvania / by Heather C. Hudak
Description: Minneapolis, Minnesota: Abdo Publishing, 2024 | Series: Haunted history of the United States | Includes online resources and index.
Identifiers: ISBN 9781098292522 (lib. bdg.) | ISBN 9798384910466 (ebook)
Subjects: LCSH: Haunted places--United States--Juvenile literature. | History--Juvenile literature. | Ghosts--United States--Juvenile literature. | Pennsylvania--History--Juvenile literature.
Classification: DDC 133.109--dc23

CONTENTS

CHAPTER ONE

STRANGE EXPERIENCES

Mark Nesbitt worked as a park ranger at the Gettysburg National Military Park in Pennsylvania for six years. During that time, Nesbitt lived in several historic houses near the battlefield. At each house, he had unusual experiences. For example, doors wouldn't stay shut even when nailed closed. But Nesbitt thought any unexplained phenomena were due to the houses' old age.

One day, Nesbitt experienced something at one historic house that was so strange he couldn't stop thinking about it. Nesbitt was

More than 165,000 soldiers fought in the Battle of Gettysburg (1863).

Some people believe the spirits of those who were not buried properly still haunt Gettysburg.

headed to the kitchen when he heard what sounded like a baby crying. The sound was so startling that Nesbitt stopped what he was doing. Since he knew he was the only person in the house, he couldn't come up with a good explanation for what the sound could be.

Nesbitt asked others who had stayed at the house if they had ever experienced anything similar. Some of them said they also had strange experiences there. Nesbitt soon discovered that the house he was living in was a short distance from the site of a former orphanage. The orphanage had housed many children who were orphaned during the American Civil War (1861–1865). Nesbitt believed the baby he heard crying was the ghost of one of the children from the orphanage.

PERSPECTIVES

WHY GHOSTS STAY

In a 2013 interview for *30 Odd Minutes*, Mark Nesbitt described why he thinks spirits continue to haunt Gettysburg more than 150 years after the fighting ended:

> ***One of the theories about why ghosts linger is because the living can't let go. You know, we can't let go of them. And 1.6 million people come every year to Gettysburg as visitors, as tourists, but basically what do they do? They mourn because they go to these sites, . . . and they think deeply about what these men suffered and did for the American people today.***

HAUNTINGS IN GETTYSBURG

The town of Gettysburg, Pennsylvania, is believed to be one of the most haunted places in the United States. The Battle of Gettysburg was fought in the town. It was one of the most important and deadliest battles of the

American Civil War. In the mid-1800s, the Northern states wanted to abolish slavery, but the Southern states wanted it to continue. War broke out over the issue in 1861 when 11 Southern states separated from the rest of the country. They were known as the Confederate States, and the Northern states were called the Union.

In 1863, the Confederate States were counting on a fast, easy win at the Battle of Gettysburg. By invading the North, they hoped to force negotiations that would end the war. From July 1 to 3, fierce fighting took place in and around the town of Gettysburg. The Union was able to hold

PARANORMAL ACTIVITY

Unusual activity that cannot be explained by science is called paranormal activity. Examples include hearing strange sounds, getting the chills, or feeling that someone else is in the room. Objects that are not where they should be and ghost sightings are other examples of paranormal activity. A survey from YouGov.com in 2021 found about 41 percent of Americans believe in ghosts.

off the invading Confederate troops, putting an end to the South's hopes of winning the war. The Confederate States lost many soldiers during the battle, and they never regained ground in the North again.

There were more than 50,000 casualties resulting from the three-day Battle of Gettysburg. Many people believe the ghosts of those who died in the battle still haunt the area today. In fact, Nesbitt is just one of countless people who believe they have had paranormal encounters in and around the town. These stories continue to draw visitors who hope to have similar experiences.

EXPLORE ONLINE

Chapter One talks about the American Civil War. The article on the website below goes into more depth on this topic. Does the article answer any of the questions you had about the war?

AMERICAN CIVIL WAR FACTS

abdocorelibrary.com/haunted-gettysburg-pennsylvania

MEADE
PENNSYLVANIA
REYNOLDS

CHAPTER TWO

GHOSTS OF GETTYSBURG NATIONAL MILITARY PARK

Much of the battlefield where soldiers fought during the Battle of Gettysburg is preserved as the Gettysburg National Military Park. The park was established in 1895 to protect significant historic lands that were part of the battle. Today, the Gettysburg National Military Park has more than 1,300 monuments, markers, and memorials. The park honors the people

The Pennsylvania Monument is the largest monument on the Gettysburg Battlefield.

PERSPECTIVES

GHOST CONCENTRATION

Stories about Gettysburg ghosts are more common in town than on the battlefield. Some people believe this is because ghost tours happen in town. Historian Tim Smith explained in a video by Adams County Historical Society that only licensed guides can run tours of the battlefield. He said, "The ghost tours are not allowed on the battlefield. And for that reason, the town is filled with ghosts, but there are very few ghosts on the battlefield." Smith also added, "Most of the stories I see mentioned didn't even come about until the late 1980s. Prior to that, there were very few, if any, true ghost stories on the battlefield. And . . . when I was young, I never heard anything about ghosts on the battlefield."

who fought and died and honors the events that took place during the battle. People also claim to have experienced paranormal reminders of the battle in many parts of the park.

During their visits to the battlefield, many people have reported seeing ghost armies marching or fighting across the battlefield. Others say they have spotted phantom riders on horseback, or they heard cannons firing and cries of pain from

Around 3,900 troops from the Confederate Army died during the Battle of Gettysburg.

injured soldiers. There are even stories of apparitions appearing in photographs of the battlefield.

IVERSON'S PITS

On July 1, 1863, Confederate Brigadier General Alfred Iverson led his brigade to attack Union soldiers at Oak Hill. On the way, they were ambushed by Union soldiers who had been hiding behind a stone wall. Just minutes later, about 900 of Iverson's troops had been shot down. The bodies of the fallen were tossed into mass trenches in the field where they were killed. Today, the area is known as Iverson's Pits. It is said to be haunted by the soldiers who died there.

In the years that followed the attack, the farmer who owned the field continued to farm the land where Iverson's Pits were dug. Many farmhands refused to work in the area after dark for fear of the spirits that roamed the land. People have reported seeing white handkerchiefs waving above the ground after dark. Others have reported seeing ghosts walking through the fields, hearing the sounds of gunfire, and seeing unexplained lights.

DEVIL'S DEN

Devil's Den is a large boulder field in Gettysburg National Military Park. It was here on July 2, 1863,

The boulders that make up Devil's Den were formed around 180 million years ago.

that nearly 8,000 Union and Confederate soldiers took part in a bloody battle. The uneven ground and sharp boulders made for a treacherous fight. There were around 2,600 casualties. Many of the bodies were not buried for days. Some were left in deep crevices among the rocks.

Today, many people visiting Devil's Den claim their electronic devices, such as cameras or phones, stop working there, even though they work in other parts of the park. Others have reported sightings of a ghost rider who is accompanied by

DEVIL'S DEN HISTORY

Even before the Battle of Gettysburg, Devil's Den had a reputation as a ghostly place. The area had been used as a hunting ground, spiritual site, and battleground. Throughout history, people have reported supernatural phenomena in the area, such as unexplained balls of light. According to legend, a huge snake lived among the boulders. Locals gave the snake the nickname "the devil." Some say that's how the area became known as Devil's Den. However, the true origins of the name remain unknown.

sounds of gunfire and shouting. He is said to disappear as quickly as he comes. One woman said a man dressed in a Civil War uniform reached up from a crevice and grabbed her ankle. By the time she called her friend over for help, the man was gone.

Several people have also claimed to see a barefoot man wearing a hat and shabby clothing at Devil's Den. He supposedly walks up to visitors, points in the distance, and tells them they will find what they are looking for over there. Then the man disappears.

FURTHER EVIDENCE

Chapter Two has information about Devil's Den. What is the main point of this chapter? What key evidence supports this point? Go to the article about Devil's Den at the website below. Find a quote from the website that supports the chapter's main point.

THE CAPTURE OF DEVIL'S DEN

abdocorelibrary.com/haunted-gettysburg-pennsylvania

Best Western
GETTYSBURG HOTEL

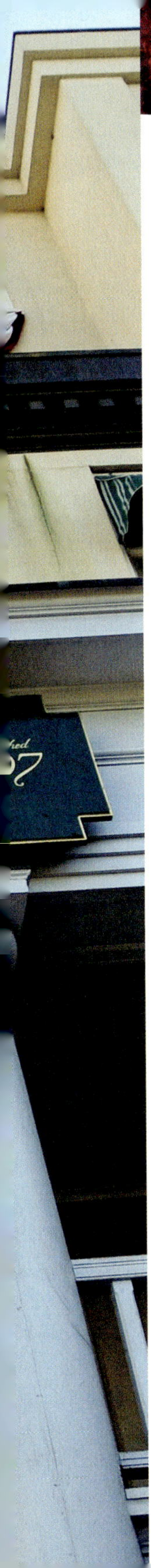

CHAPTER THREE

HAUNTED HOTELS

During the Battle of Gettysburg, farms, homes, and other buildings were used as makeshift hospitals for the wounded. Today, many of these sites are home to hotels that are believed to be haunted. The original building that houses the Gettysburg Hotel in downtown Gettysburg dates to 1797. The building started out as a tavern and was later turned into a hotel. The Gettysburg Hotel is located within walking distance of the battlefield. Thousands of

In 1983, the Gettysburg Hotel was damaged during a fire. The hotel was restored and eventually reopened in 1991.

Many barns and homes near the battlefield, such as this barn on the Codori Farm, became field hospitals during the battle.

wounded soldiers were brought to the hotel, and many died there.

Hotel guests often report mysterious events during their stays. Many have reported seeing a wounded soldier dancing with a woman in the hotel's grand ballroom. The most common supernatural sightings include a Civil War nurse known as Rachel. She wanders the halls and nearby streets searching for wounded soldiers to care for. Rachel is said to open drawers and luggage, remove items, and toss things around.

TILLIE PIERCE HOUSE INN

Tillie Pierce was a teenager when the Battle of Gettysburg took place. She witnessed the battle firsthand. Later, she wrote a book about her experiences called *At Gettysburg: What a Girl Saw and Heard of the Battle*. Wounded soldiers were brought to Pierce's family home, and she helped care for them.

Today, the house has been transformed into the Tillie Pierce House Inn. A guest room known as the Blue Room is said to be inhabited by the spirits of soldiers who died there. Some guests believe they heard what sounded like footsteps marching through the hall and in the attic above the room. Others have reported seeing a person sitting on one of the beds. There have also been many reports of a man who walks up and down the stairs as though he is keeping watch.

BALADERRY INN

In 1812, a farmhouse was built on the George Bushman farm just outside Gettysburg. Today, it is known as the Baladerry Inn. The location was used as a hospital for wounded soldiers during the Battle of Gettysburg. The spirits of seven fallen soldiers who are buried nearby are said to linger in the hallways of the inn.

One of the spirits that is said to roam the Baladerry Inn is believed to be the ghost of a Civil War nurse. Some guests have claimed to see her standing at the foot of their bed. In some cases, people said

IVERSON AT THE INN

Guests have reported seeing the ghost of Brigadier General Alfred Iverson at the Doubleday Inn. Some have even said they had a conversation with him. During the American Civil War, the land where the Doubleday Inn now stands was part of the John Forney Farm. The property saw a great deal of fighting. Iverson's Pits are located on land that was once part of the same farm. Some guests believe this is why they feel the presence of Iverson at the inn.

the nurse went through their bags. Others have heard disembodied voices, screams, and whistling. There is even a photograph of what appears to be the apparitions of two men dressed in Confederate uniforms sitting in front of the inn's French-style double doors.

FARNSWORTH HOUSE

During the Battle of Gettysburg, Confederate snipers took shelter at Farnsworth House. To this day, more than 100 bullet holes dot the walls of the hotel.

PERSPECTIVES

UNHAPPY HAUNTS

On one occasion, a local radio station held a Halloween event at Farnsworth House. Partway through the event, the phone lines went down. The crew had to run cables throughout the hotel to get the lines back up and running. Crew members were dressed in blue Civil War costumes similar to those worn by Union soldiers, and they called the radio host "the captain." Some people thought that party stirred up the Confederate spirits of the house, who believed they were under Union attack. There were dozens of ghost sightings during that one event alone.

People have reported seeing the ghosts of both Union and Confederate soldiers throughout the town of Gettysburg.

After the fighting ended, the house served as a hospital for wounded soldiers. Today, the family that owns the inn claims 16 spirits live there. Guests have reported sightings of soldiers on patrol and the sounds of footsteps, voices, breathing, and grunting.

One of the most famous spirits at Farnsworth House is known as the cranky chef. She is said to walk around the kitchen planning what to cook. She is often rude to the staff, tugging at their aprons and pushing them around. On quiet evenings, the sound of a mouth harp playing can sometimes be heard from the house's empty attic. It is believed to be the spirit of a young soldier playing at his post.

STRAIGHT TO THE SOURCE

National Geographic writer Barbara A. Noe visited Baladerry Inn. In an article, she talked about why Gettysburg is a hot spot for paranormal activity:

> *More than 7,500 soldiers died at the Battle of Gettysburg in July 1863 and were buried quickly without proper rites, many to be forgotten forever, so it's no wonder that spirits are said to roam [Baladerry Inn]—and throughout the town and the battlefield of Gettysburg. Reports of phantom apparitions, bone-tingling cries of wounded soldiers, ghostly Civil War music, even the eerie sound of horse hoofs in places where horses fell victim (apparently horses can be ghosts, too) are common.*

Source: Barbara A. Noe. "Ghosts of Gettysburg." *National Geographic*, 12 Oct. 2011, nationalgeographic.com. Accessed 3 May 2023.

BACK IT UP

The author of this passage is using evidence to support a point. Write a paragraph describing the point the author is making. Then write down two or three pieces of evidence the author uses to make the point.

CHAPTER FOUR

PARANORMAL PLACES

Beyond the battlefield and hospital inns, there are plenty of other places in Gettysburg with reported paranormal activity. Mary Virginia "Jennie" Wade was a 20-year-old seamstress at the time of the battle. Wade was staying with her sister, whose house was farther from the battlefield. But the house, now known as the Jennie Wade House, was across the street from Farnsworth House, which was where Confederate snipers were staying.

On the morning of July 3, 1863, a stray bullet from one of the snipers' rifles came

A statue of Jennie Wade stands in front of the Jennie Wade House.

REMEMBERING JENNIE WADE

Wade was the only civilian to die in the Battle of Gettysburg. She is believed to have been engaged to Corporal Johnston "Jack" Skelly at the time. Skelly died shortly after Wade. He never knew of her death. Wade is buried next to Skelly in Evergreen Cemetery, which is near the Soldiers' National Cemetery in Gettysburg. She is remembered as a hero. There is a monument that marks her grave.

through two closed doors and shot Wade in the heart. She died instantly. To this day, her bloodstains remain on the floor where she fell.

Wade's family laid her body in the basement of the house until the battle ended. Then they buried her in the yard. Months later, they moved Wade to a cemetery. Her body was moved once more after that. Some people believe her soul is still not at rest because it was disturbed so many times. Visitors to the house where Wade died claim to have seen her ghost walking the halls. Some have also reported being scratched, pushed, and pinched by someone they could not see.

Sachs Covered Bridge is another place in Gettysburg that many people believe is haunted.

DANIEL LADY FARM

The Confederate Army used what is now called the Historic Daniel Lady Farm as headquarters during the Battle of Gettysburg. When the fighting started, the barn became a field hospital for Confederate soldiers. Signs of this can still be seen to this day. A cannonball fragment remains stuck in one of the barn floor's support boards. The beams of the barn feature carvings that soldiers etched into them. Inside the farmhouse, the floors and walls still bear the blood of the wounded and dying soldiers.

Beyond the physical scars, the spirits of General Isaac Ewell and his Confederate troops supposedly patrol the area. When the Lady family came home after the battle, they found a dead soldier upstairs. This is now considered the most haunted part of the farmhouse.

PERSPECTIVES

FORENSIC TESTING

In 2007, New York detectives wanted to find out how far back photoluminescence testing could detect the presence of blood in a building. They headed to the Historic Daniel Lady Farm, which still had bloodstains from when it was used as a field hospital 140 years earlier. The equipment was able to detect bloodstains both visible and invisible to the naked eye. The discovery confirmed the importance of preserving the building as a historic landmark to remind people of the events that took place there.

NATIONAL SOLDIERS' ORPHANS' HOMESTEAD

In 1863, the National Soldiers' Orphans' Homestead was a private home. It was used as a hospital during the Battle of Gettysburg.

Some people say the spirits of children can be very playful. These ghostly children may move objects, play games, or make sounds.

Bodies of dead soldiers were placed in the home's cellar until it was safe to move them. Their spirits are said to haunt the building to this day.

Later, the building was made into an orphanage for children who had lost their parents during the American Civil War. According to some locals, one of the headmistresses at the orphanage was cruel to the children who lived there. Rumor has it that she chained them in the cellar. Some people believe her ghost is doomed to haunt the building as punishment for her evil ways. Many children went missing or died during their time at the orphanage. Visitors have reported the sounds of children's voices and chains rattling against the basement walls.

GETTYSBURG COLLEGE

Gettysburg College is located near the battlefield, and both armies used it as a field hospital. Students treated the wounded. After the battle, the college continued to be used as a hospital for the thousands of soldiers who were left behind. Many soldiers died at the college.

Since then, the college has become a hub for paranormal activity. People have reported hearing moans, screams, and cries; feeling odd sensations; or seeing spirits walking around the campus. Objects are said to go missing, and lights supposedly flicker for no known reason. Some people said they had strange experiences in one of the college's elevators. Instead of opening on the first floor, the elevator continues to the basement. When the doors open, passengers find themselves staring at ghostly surgeons performing a surgery in a gruesome Civil War-era hospital.

HAUNTED LOCATIONS IN GETTYSBURG

This map shows the locations of some of the haunted sites in Gettysburg. Why do you think these supposedly haunted locations are so close to one another?

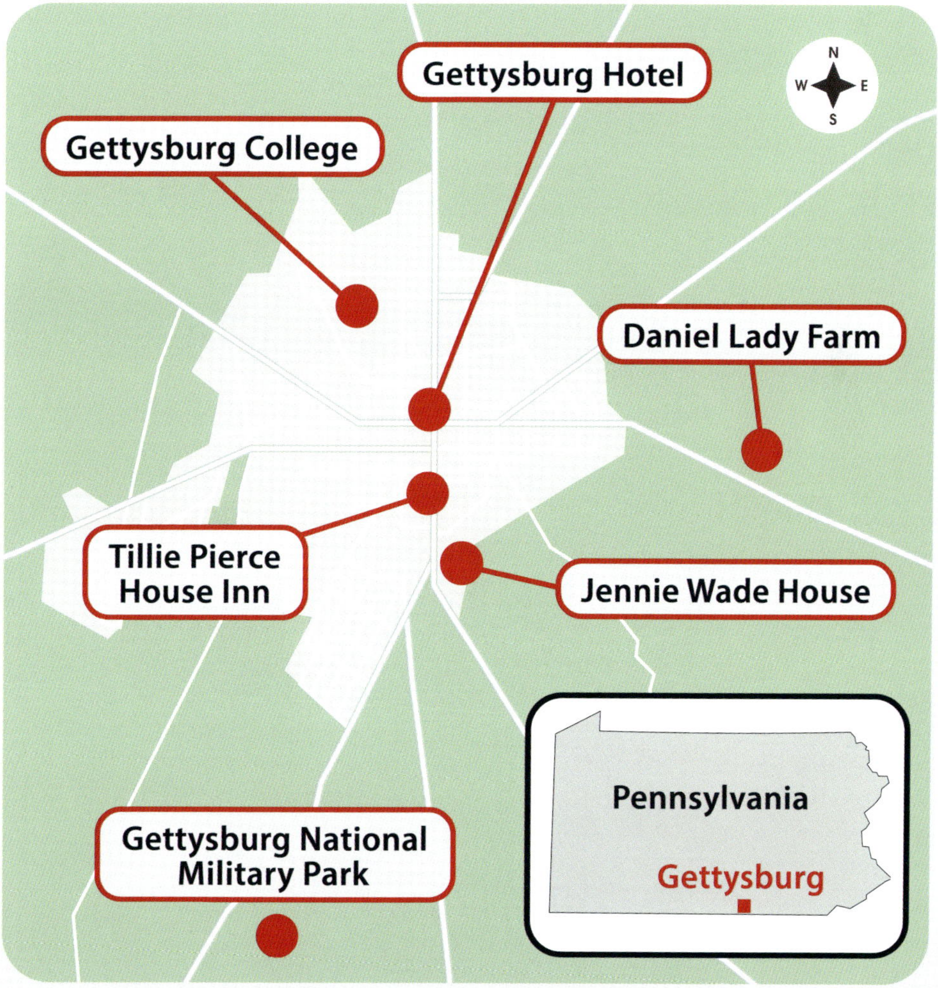

CHAPTER FIVE

EXPLAINING THE UNEXPLAINED

Ghost hunters from all over the world come to Gettysburg in hopes of encountering an apparition. Many businesses offer nighttime ghost tours to the spookiest spots in town. Some tour guides dress in period clothing and reenact scenes from the past.

After Mark Nesbitt wrote his book *Ghosts of Gettysburg* in 1991, ghost hunters from all over the world took an interest in the area. In 1994, Nesbitt created a tour company called Ghosts of Gettysburg Candlelight

A reenactment of the Battle of Gettysburg is held every year at the Daniel Lady Farm.

Walking Tours based on the ghost stories in his book. It was the first of its kind in Gettysburg. The tour company is one of the town's most popular attractions. Many other companies in the town also offer ghost tours of the area.

Several companies, such as the Gettysburg Paranormal Association, provide people with a chance to take part in a real-life paranormal investigation. Ghost hunts take place in a variety of haunted indoor and outdoor locations. Participants use special equipment, including laser thermometers, infrared cameras, electromagnetic meters, and holographic shadow detection devices, to detect the presence of spirits.

POWER OF SUGGESTION

While some people believe in the paranormal, others say there are scientific explanations for the things people experience. One explanation is the power of suggestion. People might hear that a place is haunted.

Perhaps they are given very detailed information about what they can expect to experience at a specific time or place. The suggestion is so powerful that the experience can become real for a person, even if it didn't happen.

Some experts believe this is what happens in Gettysburg. The more dramatic or convincing the storyteller, the more likely people are to see, feel, or hear what

PERSPECTIVES

GHOST TOUR TALES

On October 29, 2014, an article titled "The Specter of Gettysburg" was published in a blog known as the *Gettysburg Compiler*. In the article, student Kevin Lavery gave his perspective on ghost tours:

> ***Ghost stories are inherently dramatized and inaccurate, if not entirely fabricated. Such stories cannot possibly help to expand the public's historical consciousness in any meaningful way. At the most, these stories can provoke an interest in the past—but it is a twisted and poorly-informed interest that creates historical misunderstandings. Tour guides are storytellers, not trained historical interpreters.***

they have been told to expect. In some cases, they want to experience it, so they do.

SCIENTIFIC EVIDENCE

Science can help make sense of hauntings around Gettysburg. However, it cannot definitively confirm or disprove the presence of paranormal activity. Still, some people use tools to try to understand people's experiences.

Some scientists think infrasound might be the cause of some disembodied noises people hear at supposedly haunted sites. These sounds cannot be heard by the human ear. Air conditioners, fans, and even earthquakes can create sound energy that can't be picked up by human ears, but it may cause a strange sensation. When the source of that sound is cut off, the unusual sensation might disappear as well.

Electromagnetic waves could be another reason behind some spirit sightings. When parts of the brain are stimulated by these waves, a person sometimes

OPTICAL ILLUSION GHOSTS

Some ghost sightings can be explained by optical illusions. When an image reflects off a clear screen at a specific angle, the reflected image can look like a ghost that appears suddenly.

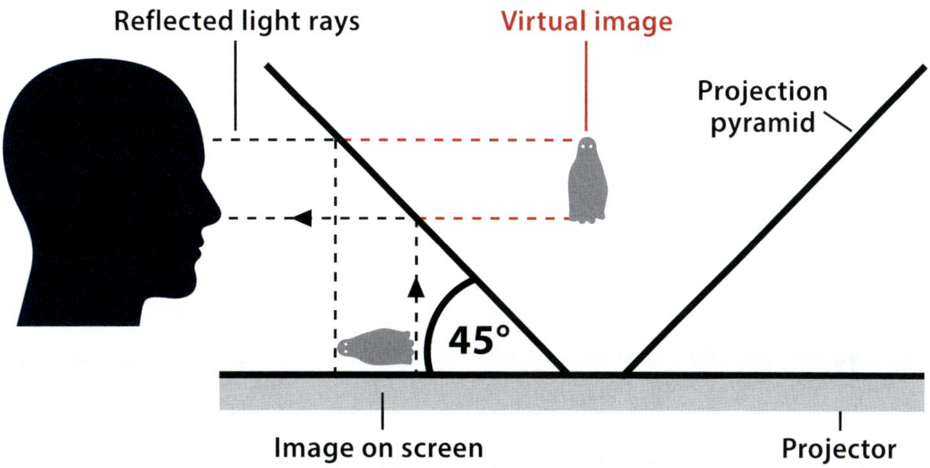

sees or feels things that aren't there. Some scientists think strong electromagnetic fields created by electronic devices, such as clocks, phones, and power lines, might contribute to the feeling that a place is haunted.

No one knows for sure if the ghosts of Gettysburg are real. However, there is no denying the horrors that took place in and around the town during the Battle of Gettysburg. With the amount of death that occurred as a result of the battle, it's easy for many people to believe there are spirits lingering in Gettysburg to this day.

GAS AND GHOSTS

Carbon monoxide (CO) may cause some people to feel as though a place is haunted. CO is a tasteless, colorless, and odorless gas. It is produced by furnaces, stoves, and other fuel-burning appliances. CO poisoning can have a strange effect on the body. Side effects include blurred vision, confusion, hallucinations, and a feeling of dread. These effects are similar to what some people say they experience in haunted buildings. Fixing a leak may put an end to these experiences.

STRAIGHT TO THE SOURCE

Ghost tour guide Mike Lyons explains what he tells people when they ask whether they will see a ghost:

> *They want to see a ghost. Come right up on the porch and they say, "If we come on your tour can you guarantee that we're going to see a ghost?" And the answer to that is "no." Can't guarantee that. Nobody can. If they do, they're lying. This house, some of the other spots near town are slightly more likely opportunities for somethin' like that to happen. You've just gotta maintain the mind and see what happens. Sometimes it does. Sometimes it doesn't.*

Source: Robert C. Thompson. "A Paradoxical Show of Hunted Ghosts and Haunted Histories." *Academia*, 2017, academia.edu. Accessed 4 May 2023.

WHAT'S THE BIG IDEA?

Take a close look at this passage. What is the main point being made about seeing spirits on ghost tours? What sort of mindset should people taking ghost tours have if they really do want to see a spirit?

FAST FACTS

- There were more than 50,000 casualties resulting from the three-day Battle of Gettysburg in 1863. The spirits of those who died are said to haunt the area to this day.
- Gettysburg National Military Park was established in 1895 to protect significant historic lands that were part of the battle. Many unexplained activities have been reported in the park since the battle.
- About 2,600 soldiers lost their lives in battle at Devil's Den in Gettysburg National Military Park on July 2, 1863. Many people have claimed to feel or see spirits, such as a barefooted man, in the area.
- Jennie Wade was the only civilian to die in the Battle of Gettysburg. She was struck by a stray bullet in her family's home. Some people believe her ghost still haunts the building she died in.
- More than 100 bullet holes from the Battle of Gettysburg dot the walls of the Farnsworth House hotel. The family that owns the hotel claims 16 spirits live there.

- Gettysburg College was used as a field hospital during the Battle of Gettysburg. Some people have reported that the elevator there skips past the first floor and continues to the basement. The doors then open into a Civil War-era hospital.
- Science can help make sense of some of the strange phenomena in and around Gettysburg. But it cannot confirm the presence of paranormal activity in the town.

STOP AND THINK

Tell the Tale

Chapter Three of this book discusses a few of the haunted hotels in Gettysburg. Imagine you are staying at one of these hotels. Write 200 words about any paranormal activity you experience during your stay. How did it make you feel?

Dig Deeper

After reading this book, what questions do you still have about the Battle of Gettysburg? With an adult's help, find a few reliable sources that can help you answer your questions. Write a paragraph about what you learned.

Take a Stand

Student Kevin Lavery believes that an emphasis on ghost stories creates a misunderstood interpretation of history. Do you think it is beneficial for ghost stories to help people who might not otherwise engage with history to learn more about the past? Or do you think misunderstandings they have because of ghost stories do more harm than good? Why or why not?

Say What?

Studying hauntings in and around Gettysburg can mean learning a lot of new vocabulary. Find five words in this book you've never heard before. Use a dictionary to find out what they mean. Then write the meanings in your own words and use each word in a new sentence.

GLOSSARY

abolish
to formally bring something to an end

apparition
a ghost or ghostlike image of a person

brigade
a subdivision of an army

casualties
people killed or injured in a war or accident

disembodied
not connected to a body

paranormal
events that can't be explained by science

phantom
a ghost or an imagined figure

photoluminescence testing
using a laser beam to detect the presence of a substance

sniper
a member of the military who can shoot targets precisely from far away

ONLINE RESOURCES

To learn more about hauntings and Gettysburg, Pennsylvania, visit our free resource websites below.

Core Library CONNECTION
FREE! COMMON CORE MULTIMEDIA RESOURCES

Visit **abdocorelibrary.com** or scan this QR code for free Common Core resources for teachers and students, including vetted activities, multimedia, and booklinks, for deeper subject comprehension.

Booklinks NONFICTION NETWORK
FREE! ONLINE NONFICTION RESOURCES

Visit **abdobooklinks.com** or scan this QR code for free additional online weblinks for further learning. These links are routinely monitored and updated to provide the most current information available.

LEARN MORE

Gale, Ryan. *Fact and Fiction of the Civil War*. Abdo, 2022.

Parker, Philip. *The Civil War Visual Encyclopedia*. DK, 2021.

Williams, Dinah. *Battlefield Ghosts*. Scholastic, 2021.

INDEX

About the Author

Heather C. Hudak has written hundreds of children's books on all kinds of topics. When she's not writing, she enjoys traveling the world and has been to nearly 60 countries. One of her favorite activities in each new city she visits is to take a ghost tour to all the most haunted places. Her most chilling experiences have been in Edinburgh, Scotland; in New Orleans, Louisiana; and aboard the *Queen Mary* in Long Beach, California.